ZERO TO CA$HFLOW

A 22 YEAR-OLD'S NO BS GUIDE TO REAL ESTATE INVESTING

KP

Zero to Ca$hflow

ZERO TO CA$HFLOW

A 22 YEAR-OLD'S NO BS GUIDE TO REAL ESTATE INVESTING

KUVAAL PATEL

KP

Zero to Ca$hflow

For permissions contact Kuvaal at email: info@kuvaal.com

Edited by Varun Patel, Lois Angelo, Dr. Jay Patel, Dr. Bina Patel, Nicole Felix-Zamora, and Niyati Patel

Contributions by Anthony Hayes Jr. and Chase Chapman

Cover Artist: Alex Funk

ISBN: 979-8-5994299-9-9

TABLE OF CONTENTS

Zero to Ca$hflow

All profit generated from *Zero to Ca$hflow* will be donated to The Gow School's general scholarship fund. The Gow School is an international boarding school that specializes in educating young men and women with learning differences. I attended Gow from ages twelve to seventeen, and it was there that I discovered my confidence and my voice.

<u>Foreword</u>

Simplicity. When Kuvaal and I began partnering in our sales businesses in 2018 he had one mission: "make it simpler."

Kuvaal Patel has an incredible ability to take complex and intricate systems and break them down into simple, easy to follow, and highly effective steps. *Zero to Ca$hflow* is yet another testament to this gift. Kuvaal has shown that no matter the field: academics, sales, or real estate he can take what others deem "confusing" or "overwhelming" and teach it to anyone.

This book will give you a step-by-step formula to increase your cash flow, start building passive income and design the life of your dreams. Kuvaal gives readers a direct look into his beginnings in real estate and his early success should inspire you that anyone with intention and clarity can go from zero to cash flowing within weeks. He reveals in this book the secrets to creating generational wealth and takes you along his path towards financial freedom from start to finish.

Zero to Ca$hflow will challenge you to think bigger, aggressively pursue your goals, and fast forward your track to success. As a colleague and one of my closest friends, I have witnessed Kuvaal do all of these things in his own life and lead his organization to do the same.

- Anthony Hayes Jr.

<u>Preface</u>

In a world where financial freedom and security are more attainable than ever before, why not go all-in? I have seen too many people working late into their lives, struggling to make it, and that is not how I picture my future. When I was 11 years old, my Middle School Headmaster told my parents that I should consider other education options if I was neither gifted, talented, nor hard-working. Thirteen months ago, I was in a mental, physical, and emotional funk that left me sitting in my office with $700 in my checking account. Today, I am a million-dollar entrepreneur, a real estate investor, and dedicated to constantly growing and evolving.

Money management is a foreign subject to those working late in their lives trying to survive. It seemed like the place I should begin. When I was 20, I closed tabs, paid for lunches, and I never asked anyone to split the bill. I had always assumed that the 'favor would be returned,' and while some people made good, most never did. At the end of 2019, my balance sheet showed my net liquid capital at a meager $2,000. While I did not incur debt, I came damn close to being a broke 21-year-old despite grossing over $150,000 that year. I began investing with my small savings accounts, and I developed a drive to learn more about my personal finances after reading Rachel Richards's *Money Honey*. We all know that if someone can't manage $100, how the hell will they manage $100,000?

I jumped into 2020 knowing that it would be a year of bold decisions. It began by connecting with an online coaching community based out of Austin, Texas to restart my fitness journey. I was hesitant to make the commitment at first but was drawn in by the business coaching included in the program. Soon after paying (and drawing my bank account to within $700), I had moments of doubt, but I knew I needed to grow. As quickly as I mentally committed, my business's revenue increased dramatically, my health and energy evolved, and I became addicted to the growth. I followed up on that feeling of success by attending Grant Cardone's 2020 Growth Convention in Las Vegas to accelerate my 2020 vision, and shortly after, the entire world came to a halt. The coronavirus pandemic resulted in businesses shutting down, major corporations filing for bankruptcy, and people not only losing their jobs but also their sanity. Mid-pandemic I began to focus on myself and my future more than ever before.

If you're reading this, I know you also want to brighten your future. Thank you for investing your time in me and in my book. My goal here is not to make money or brag about myself, but to inspire, pop fear bubbles, and show anyone how to begin a journey towards financial freedom through rental real estate. I know that there is a ton of information online, but while I was looking for myself, there was nothing out there that gave me everything I needed all in one place. I hope that this manuscript has everything needed to clear the haze and start you on your journey to passive income.

I have severe dyslexia, and honestly, I cannot read big words, so I will not include any in this book. I also do not like huge promises, so I will not include those either. I am not a real estate professional yet, but this will show you I went from knowing little about real estate to receiving my first rent check in less than three months. Buckle up, here we go.

<u>Introduction</u>

As I write this, I am 22 years old. I graduated with a Bachelor of Arts degree from the University of Arizona two years ago, at 20, and have been working in direct sales and sales management for four years. Through early-2020, I was comfortable. I had been consistently average all-around: sales revenue, level of enjoyment, and profits. When the global pandemic forced brick-and-mortar businesses to stop operations in March, I was scared to think about the future of my in-person sales team. My travels in Europe were cut short because of the international travel ban, and my business was practically shut down while I was 5,000 miles away - when I returned, the weekly sales report was a meager $300.

For context, I train and manage a team of direct salespeople that present products through one-on-one (mostly in-person, in-home) presentations. When the national shutdown began to close small companies, I expected a downturn in my business, marketing high-quality kitchen products. Surprisingly, business started to improve. We found that our target demographic began working from home, so they began cooking at home more frequently. Fast-forward four weeks, and our team was generating $25,000+ in new business weeks while working 100% online. Four weeks after that, we were consistently producing $50,000+ weeks. As my team and I began to earn more, I wanted to find a way to have my hard-earned money work hard for me, and it was then that I discovered the power of real estate.

I am studying for the California real estate salesperson exam, and am pursuing a Masters in International Real Estate at Florida International University. I specifically remember my first experience diving into this new and fantastic world; celebrating the July 4th weekend with my family, I was reading *Skip the Flip* by Hayden Crabtree (a real estate mentor). After finishing the book in two days, I began searching for my first property. I looked all over popular listing, spent hours crunching the numbers, even calling random agents, but I was not making any progress.

After my dad and I connected with a real estate investment advisor I learned that the process was much simpler than anyone made it out to be. The purpose of this book is to show you how you can do it too. You picked up this book to learn how I have residual passive income through real estate, so take what you learn from here, go out, and execute.

Zero to Ca$hflow

Timeline of My First Property

7/17 - applied for a loan on a mortgage lender's website

7/20 - uploaded financial documents to the lender's portal to be qualified for a loan

- previous 30-day pay stubs
- two months of banks statements
- last quarter of brokerage account statements
- year-to-date business profit-loss statement

7/31 - prequalified for up to $192,000 purchase price

7/31 - looked for properties within the $192,000 budget

8/5 - requested the purchase information for a single-family home - we will call this property QM for short

8/6 - made an offer to buy QM, the offer was accepted, and I was sent a purchase contract to sign

8/6 - signed the purchase contract and wired an earnest money deposit (EMD)

- EMD is a small percentage of the property's price that shows that the buyer has 'skin in the game'
- purchase contract had an estimated closing date - 9/9/2020

8/6 - shopped for home insurance (word of mouth referral)

- Emailed the insurance quote, signed purchase contract, and EMD receipt to the lender to begin loan processing

8/13 - received the home inspection report

8/15 - signed initial loan documents and faxed back

- this included the estimated interest rate and closing costs

8/18 - accepted the insurance quote from 8/7

- insurance agent sent declaration page to the lender which adds the insurance costs to amount due at closing

8/18 - contacted lender to buydown the interest rate
- we reduced the 30-year fixed rate from 4.124% to 3.499%

8/26 - updated financial documents on lender's portal
- the documents need to be refreshed to make sure the buyer can still buy every 30 days
- the underwriter is responsible for making sure a person can really afford a house

9/2 - received the final appraisal copy

9/9 - received the underwriter's final loan approval

9/11 - wired total down payment and closing costs

9/12 - signed closing documents with the notary in 35 minutes

9/14 - CLOSED!

It took less than two months to purchase an investment property from the day I applied for the loan. It took 38 days to close after finding QM. This process does not need to take months or years…when I was looking at houses online, I had no idea about what to do, but I asked many questions, did my research, and ended with the results I wanted. (feel free to reach out if you would like support: info@kuvaal.com) Let us get into the details.

<u>Chapter One</u>

Why Real Estate Investing

In February 2020, I attended Grant Cardone's 10x Growth Conference in Las Vegas. I had never heard of Grant (CEO, Founder of Cardone Capital) before going to Growth Con. Grant talked about Cardone Capital (an equity firm that enables qualified individuals to access wealth creation through real estate) and why he loves real estate. He asked all Cardone Capital investors in attendance to stand up, and Grant shared how much his company paid out in monthly distributions to those investors over the last twelve months. That's when the lightbulbs started to go off in my head. I asked my friend, Chase, who attended Growth Con with me, "Why aren't we doing this?"

Over the seven weeks prior to the conference, I had accumulated roughly $15,000 in savings. I went to a Cardone Capital representative to learn more about the investment process, but I honestly didn't ask questions - I just watched people around me throw in unfathomable sums of money. I watched one investor walk up to the table to sign a purchase contract for $250,000 and I saw a grandmother invest $80,000 into separate Cardone Capital accounts, $10,000 for each of her eight grandchildren. I also witnessed a repeat investor sign an agreement to invest another $500,000 after about 45 seconds of asking himself, "if that was enough." Finally, I decided to put $5,000, the minimum (even though it was ⅓ of my total cash at the time), into the open fund at Cardone Capital that day. After calculating the targeted return for my investment, I could expect to see a return of ~$13,000 split up into monthly distributions and the growth of the initial capital.

My very conservative circle of influence said things like, "Kuvaal, you got scammed" and "You know if they go bankrupt, you lose all that money." Some of their points had merit, and I was not even sure what was going to happen, but I had confidence. Honestly, I had zero clue what I was doing, but I found confidence in the confidence of the other investors. This is **not** smart investing, but that decision of just going for it changed my life.

When the pandemic caused an economic downturn, I began to hear the nay-sayers in my head repeating, "You know, if they go bankrupt, you lose all that money." Cardone Capital held all investor distributions for April and May as a property emergency fund, which meant that I did not get paid as quickly as I expected. But, in mid-June, distributions were sent to investors and I started to see returns. A $5,000 investment is not a lot of money in the grand scheme, but I was seeing monthly distributions - I was literally making money even while I was asleep. Think about holding real assets that appreciate in value, that are not tied to the volatile stock market, and that continue to produce a monthly cash flow forever. I like the sound of that. Do you?

There are three fundamental steps that I walk through before any buying decisions: Set my goals, determine my strategy, and plan my execution. They might sound simple, but the three steps are quite complex, and exploring them fully will help guide your real estate journey. Jot down the ideas that you think of. These three steps will help you create your Ca$hflow vision.

Chapter Two
Step 1 - Set Goals

Goals have a place in every business plan. Long term goals keep people motivated, and short-term goals drive action. There should be clearly defined goals **before** starting any endeavor. What is your real estate investing plan?

- Buy and hold rentals?
- Buy and sell in five years?
- BRRR? (Buy, Rehab, Rent, Refinance, then Repeat)
- Flip houses?
- House hack?

There are many different ways to succeed in real estate. Invest the effort and time to research different paths, and then set your goals to guide long term achievements and drive short term action. To set my short-term goal, I asked myself, "How soon do I want to own a property?" My answer was by my 23rd birthday (about three months from when I got serious about buying real estate). My long-term goal is to own a ten-property portfolio by the end of 2022.

What are your financial goals? Do you want to supplement your full-time income? Do you want to 'retire' early? A cash flowing real estate portfolio, with the proper income tax preparations, can financially retire a person or family in just a matter of years. My long-term financial goal is to have a portfolio that creates passive cash flow pay for my lifestyle expenses. To break it down and drive action, my short-term goal is to own a real estate portfolio that generates $3,000 in monthly cash flow by the end of 2021.

Be aware that goal setting may make you nervous at first, but when you discover what resonates it will light you up! There are no wrong answers when it comes to setting goals, but I have found that proper goal setting helps drive short-term actionable steps to success.

Chapter Three
Step 2 - Determine Strategy

After gaining clarity with your goals, it is time to determine the strategy to accomplish them. I picked rental properties as my strategy, but starting out, I was not sure if I wanted to purchase a multifamily or single-family property, and I did not know which market I wanted to buy-in.

I was contemplating purchasing property near where I live in California but discovered some drawbacks. California is a tenant-friendly state. I wanted to own rental properties in a landlord-friendly state. When people picture the potential negatives in rental real estate, one of the most common things they think of is a grueling tenant. In landlord friendly states, there is less tolerance for lousy tenants breaching their leases - if a tenant does not pay rent, has pets against the agreement, or breaches another part of the lease, there are fewer required notices to begin the eviction process compared to a tenant-friendly state.

I also found that Los Angeles has a rent-to-value ratio (a property's monthly rent compared to the property's value) that was not ideal for my goals. Achieving a minimum 1% rent-to-value ratio is my benchmark when measuring cash flow. If the property is worth $100,000, then, ideally, I want monthly rent to total at least $1,000. In most cases, the ratio in Los Angeles is poorly skewed because of the high land value compared to the value of the improvements (built structures), so it poorly skews the rent-to-value ratio. A multifamily property was listed for $1,699,000 (just the land itself was worth $1,200,000), with a projected rent of around $9,500. This rent-to-value ratio is 0.55%; to achieve the 1% rule the monthly rent should be ~ $17,000. A lower rent-to-value ratio does not mean that this property is a bad investment, it just does not align with my investment goals. I decided that the most efficient way to hit my goals was to look out-of-state.

Another component to determine strategy is financing. Most people only know about conventional financing with 20% down, and this is why many people believe that they need hundreds of thousands saved just to buy real estate. Conventional loans can close with as low as a 3% down payment but note that anything under 20% down will result in private mortgage insurance (PMI). PMI is a non-negotiable fee that buyers pay to protect the bank against loan defaults. The fee for PMI is a percentage of the loan amount. But, because of the additional fee some people are scared that PMI makes for a poor investment. In my opinion, if someone is able to save thousands in tied-up capital with a smaller down payment and use that money in other investments, where the returns outweigh the costs of PMI, then paying for PMI is totally worth it.

There are two commonly known benefits that come from holding rental properties. The first is appreciation, or how much the value of the property increases over time. Think back to the grandmother who put $80,000 into Cardone Capital. She wants to help her grandchildren have money for their future. That $10,000 is expected to appreciate greatly over time. The other is cash flow, or how much profit a property generates. To calculate cash flow, combine all of the property's rent and subject all of its expenses.

My long-term goal is to have all of my lifestyle expenses paid for by my real estate portfolio, so I am focused on cash flow investing. Appreciation is great, and it happens faster in growing markets, but I did not want to bank on the value of a property increasing over time for me to see a return on investment. Hayden's *Skip the Flip* mentions that investing solely based on a high appreciation potential is like roulette gambling. It could land on black or red, but, realistically, we do not have much control over it. Focusing on one or the other depends on what the investor wants to see from their investments. Combining decent cash flow and decent appreciation is a great formula.

After understanding the above, I decided the best strategy would start with purchasing single-family homes in a strong cash flow market. Strategy set!

Zero to Ca$hflow

Chapter Four
Step 3 - Plan it Out

As the saying goes, "if you fail to plan, you plan to fail." My plan to create lifestyle cash flow includes buying 'x' number of properties with certain cash flow criteria by date 'y'. Part of this plan includes assembling a team, and through my word-of-mouth advertising experience in direct sales, I was introduced to a helpful lender, great insurance agents, knowledgeable tax accountants, and property managers. You can find great people as well, just reach out to anyone you know (and trust) in real estate! This can be a local realtor, a family friend, or the guy who wrote this book.

The people on your team do what they do to serve the consumer; make sure to choose and use them wisely - an experienced group of individuals will generally increase chances of success and shorten your learning curve. Real estate agents and other service providers that you meet but do not end up working with at first could be the people you work with in the future, so maintaining relationships is important. When I started looking for properties, I was searching in Phoenix without any real criteria. I connected with an agent to help me look, but after a few days, I realized that I needed to invest elsewhere, so I let her know. I am confident that when I do work in Phoenix, she will be top of my list.

Have a clear-cut exit strategy. Some people buy and hold a portfolio for a long time, others buy and sell to 'upgrade.' Depending on your goals, risk tolerance, and knowledge, any exit path is viable, but an exit strategy is going to help expedite your decision making and guide you. Knowing what is going to happen in the future by working backward to today helps create a long-term vision and plan.

<u>Chapter Five</u>
Organizing Finances

In 2020, interest rates were at an all-time low. The historical average mortgage interest rate is roughly 8%, and there were times (many years ago) where people were even ecstatic about a 15% interest rate. I secured a 30-year fixed mortgage with a 3.499% interest rate, which is a great rate for a conventionally financed out of state investment property. Mortgage rates are determined by many factors, including the loan type and borrower's creditworthiness and financial situation. Now, if we compare the average rate of inflation to some 2020 interest rates, it almost seems like people are getting "free money." I have even connected with people who have gotten interest rates around 2%.

To be preapproved means that an expert has looked through an individual's financials and says that this person is able to purchase property up to 'x' amount. A buyer does not need to be preapproved for a loan before they shop, but from my market research and experience, being preapproved is the most efficient way to shop. Some sellers might not consider an offer without prequalification, and some agents will not work with a buyer unless they are prequalified.

The preapproval process is simple, and it will give a buyer a budget to keep in mind while they are shopping. I was scouring websites for $300,000 multi-unit properties, and a few weeks later, I was preapproved for a max purchase price of $192,000. This means that I could buy any combination of properties at the same time as long as they added up to, or were less than, $192,000. Ask your underwriter or lender if there are different things you can do to increase the preapproved purchase amount, and do not forget to explore different loan types and lender options.

To begin the prequalification process, I was asked to submit the following documents:

1. Previous two years tax returns
   - This is 2020, and in 2018 my adjusted gross income ('AGI,' total gross income minus specific deductions) was roughly $19,000. This is NOT impressive, so, in addition to my 2018 tax return, I also included a year-to-date 2020 profit-loss statement for my business.
2. Last 30-day pay stubs
3. Previous two months bank and brokerage account statements
4. A copy of my driver's license
5. Signed approval to pull my official credit report

Let's break down the necessary documents. The previous tax returns show a stable history of employment and income. However, an individual does not always need two or three years of tax returns. For example, if someone obtained a degree and is working in the same industry that they studied, they are able to use education as a form of work history.

Pay stubs from the previous 30 days show steady income and verify employment.

The previous bank statements show monthly expenses and a history of deposits which is used to verify proof of funds. If a buyer would like to put 20% down on a 100k home, the lender wants to make sure that they have at least $20,000 liquid available.

The brokerage accounts show the lender how much a buyer has in reserves.

Finally, the credit score authorization lets the lender see an official credit report and payment history. The lender can see if a borrower has any missed or late payments. The credit report is one of the most important documents when applying for a new loan. This is generally a holistic view of someone's financial DNA.

Theoretically, people can be preapproved for a loan that is 5x their income, unless there are major debts or red flags in their credit history. Once preapproved, the buyer will get a letter from the lender that confirms they are approved for a purchase price up to a certain amount. This is valid with sellers for two to three months barring any financial pitfalls.

What happens if someone does not get preapproved? There are three options that come to mind. First, explore other types of financing. Second, partner with someone in a better financial position. Or third, sort out personal finances.

Zero to Ca$hflow

Chapter Six
Shopping

I love looking at pictures of homes online and seeing them in person. Knowing a preapproved budget expedites the process by excluding the homes that are out of budget. Some factors that could go into which property you choose to buy include:

- Location
- Renter/Owner breakdown of the area
- Size (Single Family Residence or Multi-unit)
- Neighborhood grade
- Potential rent-to-value ratio
- Age of the house (and of its insides)
- Expenses (insurance, taxes, potential costs for repairs)
- Occupancy rate
- Jobs or job growth in the area

Why is location important? Some investors only purchase real estate within 200 miles of where they live, so they can easily drive-in case they are needed. Others invest 100% out of their state. Inside a city there are different markets, and each market has individual characteristics. If someone is considering buying property in Los Angeles, they need to be more specific. There are big differences in the South LA market compared to the Beverly Hills market. The demographic breakdown of an area, the school system, jobs, and crime rates are all important things to consider when considering different locations.

Why is size important? A single-family home relies on one source of rent, whereas a multifamily property relies on multiple sources of rent. I am a fan of both sizes, but I know some people who only buy multifamily properties and others who only buy single family.

What is a neighborhood grade? Neighborhoods are usually graded on an A to F scale where A class areas are generally very affluent, and C class areas are more 'working class.' Through my experience, I have found the best returns for my goals in B-class or C-class neighborhoods, but again, I have met people who only buy in A-class areas. Obviously keeping your property in a safe area affects the rentability and rental value, but I encourage you to explore the market more and find the pockets of great returns!

Why does a property's age matter? There is a lot that goes into building a home, from the foundation to the ceiling and everything in between. Older homes that have not been renovated could have major structural or mechanical flaws. Needing to replace a roof, switch out a water tank, or redo a foundation could lead to huge repair bills (impacting cash flow), and these repairs are commonly needed in older properties. New construction homes might include a home warranty where the out-of-pocket repair costs for the first few years are nominal. In general, new construction homes will not have much, if any, repair expenses over the short term, and most developers charge a premium because of that.

A property's taxes and insurance are very important when determining the return on investment. I looked at purchasing a multifamily home in Orange County, about 45 minutes away from where I live, and the numbers did not make sense when I added in the taxes and insurance. In Jackson, Mississippi, where I own my rental properties, the property taxes are less than $100 a month. In comparison, the lowest property taxes for some multifamily properties in Orange County that I saw were $450 a month!

The occupancy rate is the percent of properties that are tenanted compared to what is available. If a market has a 50% occupancy rate that means that half of the available properties are looking for a tenant, which suggests that the area is not desirable. Some markets have an occupancy rate between 95% and 100%, where property managers have a waiting list of potential renters. To see if an area is desirable or is not desirable go to an online rental website and filter only properties for rent. If you find an area that does not have many listings, then the rentals in that area are in very high demand.

Job growth helps determine if a market is healthy. Inglewood, California is a great example. Inglewood has not been talked about as the nicest place to live; however, the two new stadiums (SoFi and Inglewood Basketball and Entertainment) have created thousands of jobs. Many people will be moving to Inglewood for work, creating a massive demand for rental properties.

If you need help finding a property, or you feel like all the good deals are taken before you get to them, you are probably correct! You are not the expert here, and neither am I. The best deals are always found through people! These could be referred to as pocket listings, where the seller does not market the property on the Multiple Listing Services (MLS is an online listing website that only real estate professionals have access to). If a buyer is local to a market that they want to invest in, they could drive around (referred to as 'driving for dollars' in the real estate community) and look for great properties that you can add value to (like a distressed house) or even those properties with a "for sale by owner" sign. A property generally becomes distressed if the owner cannot keep up with the payments, and in many cases, distressed properties lack visual appeal. They might have an overgrown lawn, a visibly cracked foundation, or a tarp over the top to cover a sunken roof. Distressed property owners might not be able to make payments, or just might abandon the property.

Start to network! Tell your friends and family what you want to do because they could know someone who could help. Researching and networking helped me find the company that I would purchase my first property from. I spoke with more than 30 property owners and real estate agents in a two-week period before I decided to purchase QM. I was looking all over the country in different markets and at different types of properties.

When shopping for properties, make sure to complete due diligence. My first property had $775 as the listed rent, but after closing and talking to property management, I realized that the rent was $650 and would increase to $775 at the start of the new lease term. Ask for a copy of the current lease agreement and the last 24 to 36 months of lease agreements to confirm the rental income and the rent increases. The projected rent could be different from the actual rent, and the different amounts could determine the decision to purchase or negotiate. Use a *pro forma* to calculate the Internal Rate of Return (IRR) and the Cash-on-Cash returns based on the estimated sales price, loan costs, rent, and expenses. IRR is the total return of the entire investment while Cash on Cash returns calculates the amount of cash flow compared to how much money was initially invested.

All of these notes will help determine which property you will purchase but remember — it only works if you work. Put time into your schedule to be able to research markets and properties. You have a lot of information, so now go out and find your property.

Zero to Ca$hflow

<u>Chapter Seven</u>
Offers and Underwriting

There are two ways to purchase a property. The most common way to purchase is to finance a property, borrowing someone else's money to buy and repaying the principal amount with interest. Some examples are conventional financing (when someone borrows from a major bank), government-backed loans (Federal Housing Administration loan), or private money (also known as 'hard money.' Sourced from a private individual or private corporation, carrying a much higher interest rate). A less common financing is a seller-financed deal, where the seller creates the mortgage terms, and the buyer sends monthly payments to the seller. The second way to purchase a property is all-cash. Simply put, a buyer sends the agreed-upon sales price in full to the seller — no financing is used.

When it is time to make the offers, submit a letter of intent (a formal offer to purchase the property for a specific price) to the seller. Remember, it does not hurt to negotiate. There are some pocket listings (the best deals kept off big listing services) that get snatched up within minutes of being 'for sale.' On the flip side, there are properties that are sitting on the market for months where the owner could be very open to negotiating the price to get rid of the property.

Once an offer is accepted then the buyer will send the earnest money and get the signed purchase contract off to the lender to begin the loan processing. The earnest money deposit shows the seller that a buyer has skin in the game. The EMD for QM was only $1,000, and this goes toward the total costs at closing. The EMD is sent to escrow, a third party who exists to verify the source of funds, and they hold funds until all conditions of closing have been completed. At this point, the buyer's bank accounts, and credit report are being watched like a hawk, so they should not apply for any forms of credit (cards, cars, or other loans) or have extremely large transactions on their account.

My company gives managers a car allowance to lease a BMW. I wanted to begin car shopping in August, and I was looking at the 2020 430i convertible. I was excited to lease the car, but I had to wait until after closing the house to let BMW run my credit. A credit check mid-closing could decrease an investor's credit score and make them look riskier, changing the terms of the mortgage. I signed all of the mortgage closing documents on a Saturday morning. The bank and lender needed time to record the sale, but right after the loan was funded on Monday, I was on the phone with BMW to finalize my lease. If I let BMW run my credit too early, then closing QM could have been delayed.

Do not change your financial situation mid-closing. Some financial variables that could delay closing are:

- Changing or leaving jobs
- Buying or leasing a car

- An increase to any major payment (rent, car, etc.)
- Applying for a credit card or other types of loans
- Random large deposits or withdrawals

Should one of these things happen, the underwriter will request all documentation and ask for an explanation.

<u>Chapter Eight</u>
Interest Rates

I have found that numbers turn people off, but this is really where you want to tune in… trust me. Currently, we are seeing interest rates at all-time lows. An interest rate is a percent of the loan amount that is charged as a borrowing fee (cost to borrow money). I like the idea of a 20% down payment for a conventional loan, but everyone has different preferences and risk tolerances. If I were to purchase a $100,000 property, I would down $20,000 (20% of the price) as a down payment. The remaining $80,000 is paid to the seller, by the lender, upon closing, and I have to pay the lender the $80,000 plus interest over a specified number of periods.

A handful of factors determine what rates a buyer can get. The riskier the situation, the higher the interest rate.

- Credit score
  - A credit score lets lenders know how financially responsible a person is.
  - A higher credit score deems a borrower worthy of a lower interest rate; it is a reward for being financially responsible.
- The property variables
  - What is the value of the property?
  - What is the loan amount?
  - How much is the down payment?
  - Is it a second home, primary home, or investment property?
- What are the terms to the loan?
  - Fixed or adjustable? Fixed rates stay the same while adjustable rates may start fixed but could fluctuate up/down based on market rates.
  - Longer payback period or shorter payback period?
  - Conventional loan, FHA, or another type of loan?

Intentionally lowering an interest rate by paying an upfront fee is referred to as "buying down the interest rate." The fee to buydown is a small percent of the total loan amount. A single percent is referred to as 'a point.' In this example, the loan amount is $80,000 (put down 20% of a $100,000 home), and the loan document has 5% listed as the interest rate. If the lender says that it will cost one point to buydown the interest rate by a half-point, then paying 1% of $80,000 ($800) will buy the interest rate down to 4.5%. Calculate the total returns with each situation by adding the proposed fee into the closing costs and a lower interest rate into the monthly payments.

The initial loan documents that the lender will send include an estimated interest rate. If a buyer likes the rate, they can lock it in, so it does not change by the time of closing. I called my lender to lock in the original rate for QM's loan (4.124%), but we looked at options to buydown the rate. On that phone call, I decided to spend an additional $350 to buydown the rate from 4.124% to 3.499% so over the life of the loan I would save over $7,000.

Interest rate	Principal + Interest over 30 yr. fixed
4.124%	$269 / month = $3,228 / year = **$96,840**
3.499%	$249 / month = $2,988 / year = **$89,640**
Total saved =	**$7,200**

Once a loan rate is locked in there is a 60-day limit on how long that rate will be valid. If 60 days pass and the loan has not closed, there will be a fee to continue to lock the previous rate in, or the rate will be whatever the market determines.

<u>Chapter Nine</u>
Home Inspection and Appraisal

An inspector will visit the property and write a report on its insides and outsides. The inspector reports the estimated age of the roof, water heater, HVAC system, and anything else that might need to be repaired eventually. Roofs need to be replaced every two decades and water heaters need to be replaced every 8-12 years. If these things are near the end of their lives, a new owner may have costly repairs in their future.

During this home inspection process, there may be additional, specialized inspections (a termite inspection, for instance) that might take place. These inspections are very important. If the property needs to have many items addressed, it might delay closing or be a relatively large expense for the seller or buyer. The seller has the option to fix the problem or sell the property "as-is," which could open the door to negotiating.

QM's home inspection report listed every piece of equipment and every structural component with a photo and a grade. They graded each area with 'Satisfactory,' 'Marginal,' 'Repair or Replace,' or 'Further Evaluation' as the guide. Be careful to look at each part of your inspection report so you know exactly what type of project you could be getting into.

After the inspection, the property is "appraisal ready." Punctuality in the housing market is a foreign language, and the real estate world is very busy with the volume of pending transactions, so getting everything done on-time is difficult. Appraisals are coordinated by the lender and the seller and may take a few weeks to be completed.

The appraisal report includes everything from lot size to detailed square footage of the subject property and all of the comparable properties. It is important to read this in detail, because the property's appraised value is buried in this report. A buyer can renegotiate or back out of the contract if the appraisal comes back lower than the agreed upon sales price (a buyer would not want to pay $10 if it is only worth $5). If the appraisal comes back high, then the buyer got a deal! QM appraised $500 over the agreed sales price. The appraisal report might include more pictures of the home and receipts of recent work orders. It will also include details of the surrounding area, from the construction of the neighborhood to what soil is below the house. While it might seem over the top, there might be some important details to review.

Zero to Ca$hflow

Chapter Ten
Closing

Closing is the last step in purchasing a home! After everything is approved by the buyer and seller, all that is left is the underwriter's final approval. The underwriter will look through all of the documents (including the buyer's financials, the inspection report, and the appraisal) to give their final approval.

There is a mandatory three-day waiting period between the final underwriter approval and being able to sign the final closing documents with a notary. This waiting period is to ensure every party has enough time to review the details of the closing documents and make an appointment with a notary. A notary acts as a witness for the signing. This is the time when the down payment and closing costs are wired to the appropriate place. Once notarized, the closing documents are submitted, and the loan is closed. CONGRATULATIONS!

According to a Realtor.com article, the average closing takes fifty days. Some closings take over three months while others take 30 days! My first closing took 38 days from start to finish. I closed on my first property on 9/14, nine days before my birthday goal, and my property was rented out and cash flow positive starting from day one.

<u>Chapter Eleven</u>
Property Management

I know some investors that enjoy managing their own property, and others who outsource those duties to a property management company. Ask yourself if you value the time spent managing the property as much as you value the other work that you do. If you feel like others can add more value than you, outsource to a professional.

How can you maximize your time for the maximum return? As a real estate investor, your first priority is to find more deals to add to your portfolio. I feel that giving my properties to a property management company shortens the learning curve and frees up more time. The time spent talking to a tenant about a problem and organizing a technician to come by could be better spent in other ways to build your portfolio. Some property management companies charge a flat monthly fee, others charge a percentage of rent (usually 6% to 12%). The right property management is worth every penny for me. It frees time, stress, and hassle so I can focus on creating more opportunities.

The property management agreement (PMA) will include the scope of work outlining the duties of the property management group. A property manager could be in charge of finding and screening tenants, collecting rents, handling complaints, and fixing issues that may arise. Once the property is in the very capable hands of the property manager, it is all ready to start generating cash flow. As Grant Cardone says, "cash is trash, cash flow is king."

Chapter Twelve
Round Two

A week after QM closed, I wanted to jump right into the second property. Generally speaking, as long as your other properties are tenanted, you have no major change to your debt-to-income ratio, and the monthly expenses of the properties are less than 75% of the rental income you, theoretically, could be prequalified for another conventional mortgage of the same purchase price.

QM closed at 9 A.M. and that BMW I had my eye on was mine by 4 P.M. that afternoon. Even though my company has a car allowance to pay for the BMW, there needs to be two years of receipts to not affect my debt-to-income ratio. Because I did not have two years of receipts, my debt-to-income ratio was demolished, and instead of prequalifying for another $192,000 purchase price, I prequalified for up to $92,000.

We found a potential second property about a week after QM closed. I signed the purchase contract and submitted the earnest money deposit to begin round two, but a few hours later we found a title issue with the property. A common cause for a title issue is a property lien (i.e., the current owner owes someone money). To resolve title issues could take weeks or months, so instead of waiting for the issue to clear, we voided the purchase contract and restarted the search for a new property.

A week later we found the next property, and I signed the purchase contract. This closing had more headaches than QM's closing. With the winter weather, there were many delays with the rehab work. The inspection and appraisal were over 45 days late. I was blessed with a hiccup-free QM closing. I was spoiled! I heard that "everyone loses something on their first deal, but it is the value of the learning opportunity that makes it worth it." In my case, I did not lose anything in deal number one, but I did lose a lot of time in deal two.

Seeing the differences in each deal has been eye-opening, and that quote is somewhat correct. The opportunity I have had to learn from the second property has been well worth it.

Zero to Ca$hflow

Chapter Thirteen
Different Loan Types

After learning more about leverage, I learned that there are many ways to use other people's money in real estate, referred to as OPM. It is important to not over-leverage, but as long as a debt is used to create wealth, it is a 'good debt.' Financing cars or buying overpriced computers is 'bad debt,' also known as consumer debt.

While I am still new to real estate, I do not see any real estate investment loan as being bad debt, it just depends on the numbers. Cardone Capital has a decent amount of debt, but that debt is used to purchase wealth-creating assets. Using leverage to put down as little money as possible on a property that brings in monthly cash flow to reinvest is the goal of investors, and there are many types of loans that someone could use to purchase real estate. Whichever loan an individual gets depends on their situation.

Conventional Loan

Conventional loans are the most common. With this loan, people are used to hearing "20% down, 20% down, 20% down." In practice, it is possible to obtain conventional financing with as little as 3% down. With less money down the monthly principal and interest payments are higher but could be worth it if a buyer qualifies for a 2-3% interest rate. Loans with less than 20% down payment have a PMI which adds a monthly fee until an owner has roughly 20% equity (See Chapter 3: Step 2 if you need a refresher). The Homeowners Protection Act requires lenders to remove the PMI once the loan to value is between 78% - 80%. Loan-to-value (LTV) means how much debt is on the home compared to the ownership (equity). If a buyer puts 20% down, the LTV is 80%. If they put 3.5% down, the LTV is 96.5%. Each monthly payment contributes to the equity the owner has in the home.

In a fully amortized loan, let us say the monthly payment is $500. The first $500 payment will be split, so almost all of the payment goes towards paying the interest back to the bank with a very small amount going towards equity of the property. As a rule of thumb, the bank always wants to make sure they get paid back first. It could be split into $0.15 toward the principal of the loan and $499.85 to pay off the interest, for example. As someone gets further and further into their payments, the split decreases until the end of the period (15 or 30 years usually) when the final payment might be $499.90 toward the principal and $0.10 toward the interest.

FHA Loan

FHA loans are government-backed loans that allow buyers to purchase a home with as little as 3.5% down. These loans have a lower credit score requirement, better interest rates compared to conventional loans, and have lower mortgage insurance rates (similar to a PMI but called a Mortgage Insurance Premium [MIP] for FHA loans).

These loans are only for owner-occupied properties. A common misconception is that an individual is only allowed to have one FHA loan ever, but in practice, it is only one active FHA loan at any one time. After some mortgage payments and equity appreciation, FHA owner-investors could refinance their FHA loan to a conventional loan, allowing them to open another FHA loan. Then that first home could be a full rental property. This is a great way to save large amounts of money upfront and still get a great property.

Other Options

There are many other financing options like balloon mortgages, adjustable-rate loans, VA loans, and USDA loans. Each has respective pros and cons. Private money is also an option. Private money loans are generally shorter-term loans with much higher interest rates. These are not fulfilled by banks or credit unions but by private lenders, and private money loans could be 'easier' to get because there is less bureaucracy. They can be funded relatively quickly. Generally, the property being bought is used as collateral in private money situations. Private money is very common in real estate investing with high caliber investors. Flippers commonly use private money because they can get the money fast to close a purchase very quickly. They do their rehab work in a few months and sell the house quickly. The lump profit they can make from a flip with the quick ability to fund a loan is worth the higher interest rates.

Zero to Ca$hflow

Chapter Fourteen
Lessons Learned

This chapter is dedicated to my friend Steven Lewis of the Steven Lewis Group at EXP Realty. While at a professional coaching event in Austin, Texas in October 2020, I met Steven. We spoke about FHA loans and how lucrative that could be with 'house-hacking.' He changed my perspective on real estate investing.

FHA loans allow for more leverage but have to be owner-occupied. As I am writing this, there is a duplex for sale in Bakersfield, California for $150,000. If I put down 3.5%, including closing costs, the total upfront cost would be close to $10,000. I would have an estimated monthly payment, including interest, taxes, and insurance, of $800. The average rent in Bakersfield, according to a quick Google search, is $1,064. Even if I receive slightly below average rent ($900) for one unit that would cover the house payment and cash flow $100! I am being paid $100 to own and live in the property. After a few years of mortgage payments, cash flow, and property appreciation, we could refinance the loan from an FHA loan to a conventional loan, which would allow me to rent the second unit, adding another source of monthly rental income ($900) into the cash flow mix. After refinancing, I am able to secure another FHA loan.

If I were to restart, I would use Steven's house hacking method to purchase a property using an FHA loan, maximizing the capital and potential leverage. As shown in the basic example above, it would cost me less upfront, and after a few years of living in a property that I own, it would start cash flowing nicely.

Thank you for mentoring me, Steven! I appreciate you taking the time to share your knowledge after only meeting once. Big things are coming for us!

Chapter Fifteen
Final Thoughts

There are a handful of things that property owners do to ensure long-term success in real estate, like working with asset protection lawyers to draw up estate plans and generate long term wealth and tax strategies. The most common forms of asset protection are moving rental properties into limited liability companies (LLCs) or purchasing an umbrella insurance policy to protect your assets from potential lawsuits.

My property management company recommends that I keep my real estate business income and expenses separate from my other businesses to be able to classify it accurately for taxes. In *Rich Dad Poor Dad,* Robert Kiyosaki mentions that real estate investors take full advantage of the tax codes and pay less in taxes than most people think. When someone understands that the tax code is a 'play book' on how to create wealth, they are able to adjust their strategy to elevate their success.

What about the cash flow? My favorite part! When properties are tenanted, a property manager will collect rent checks, pay the expenses, and send the excess cash flow to the owner. If your loan does not have a prepayment penalty and you have excess cash flow, you could pay off the mortgage early. Use online calculators to see how much you could save in interest by paying more, and also consider what you could do with the cash flow if it was not put into the payment. In my case, I would much rather have the cash available to invest in other things.

I received the first rent check for my property two weeks after I closed. It felt incredible to think that I will continue to have that feeling for as long as I hold the property. Rents generally increase every year, but mortgage payments stay the same. If the 30-year fixed monthly payment is $350 in 2020, in 2050 that payment is still $350. However, the 2020 monthly rent of $775 could easily be over $2,000 by 2050. Hard work may pay immediately, but hard-working money will pay indefinitely. Thus, creating wealth.

What is next for me? My goal is ten properties by the end of 2022. Based on my math, the cash flow of ten properties would cover all of my monthly expenses. Knowing myself, I would continue to work, but this would give me peace of mind and would afford me the opportunity to focus on other interests.

Writing this short book has been very enjoyable, and it's been a sincere joy to be able to share the simple steps to invest in real estate. I am also excited to create an organization in the near future and allow investors to invest in a real estate portfolio alongside me. I enjoy finding deals, analyzing numbers, and doing the work. I want to help the people around me invest in real estate; this industry is the financial freedom answer for many, and we are barely scratching the surface.

I hope that now you can see the simplicity of buying real estate. While nothing is 'easy,' I strongly believe that this entire process is simple. Qualify, shop, organize, be diligent, and close.

If it seems 'too easy to be true,' reread this book. I went from

zero to real estate investor in less than two months, and anyone

else can too.

My one ask of each reader - share this with someone you

know will get value from it. Every purchase and share of this

book helps grow the general scholarship fund for students with

learning differences. Operate with abundance. I know that there

is enough success in this world for you, me, and everyone

around us — that is why I am writing this book. I know that not

every reader will actually take action, because it might be scary

or overwhelming. I also know that those that do will create long

lasting freedom and security. If I am able to succeed, then it is

my duty to allow the people around me to succeed as well. I hope

that with the knowledge that you have gained through my story

and my experience you can open the door and spread the wealth.

<u>Afterword</u>

Do you ever just think "Real estate investing sounds great, but it looks too confusing?" If you answered yes to some variation of this question, congratulations you are not alone! In a world where information is plentiful & easily accessible, it can be tough to find reliable information that is easy to understand. Even with all the information, do you know what to do with it?

Kuvaal has made a successful career of being able to turn the difficult concepts into easy-to-follow instructions. Where a lot of people tend to hide behind big vocabulary words to sound intelligent, Kuvaal's intelligence is validated through his simple explanations and being intentional with his actions.

Kuvaal and I have been friends/colleagues for a few years, during which we bonded over the fact that so many people have this longing desire to build wealth and be successful but often feel stuck or discouraged because they don't know how to get started or what questions to even ask. Kuvaal's gift is to be able to bridge that gap. Kuvaal's magnetic personality will have you feeling empowered that investing in real estate is possible for you. They say knowledge is power when action is taken, let this book provide you the knowledge and the jumpstart to take action.

Kuvaal's conversational and easy to read book, *Zero to Ca$hflow*, is a testament that the world of investing in real estate doesn't just have to be reserved for the old & wealthy but that with hard work and an eagerness to learn, you too could go from *Zero to Ca$hflow*.

Everyone starts somewhere, so stop waiting & just start.

- Chase Chapman

Buying homes at twenty-two & so can you!

This is a step-by-step guide on how I purchased my first real estate investment property and created multiple passive-residual-streams of income through real estate at the age of 22.

I went from basic real estate knowledge to earning my first rent check in less than 3 months. Learn from my success and what I wish I'd known at the time.

If you have considered investing in real estate, but the huge promises, overcomplicated steps, or massive dollar amounts have intimidated you, I got your back. Financial freedom and security are now more attainable than ever before.

In a quick read, learn how to:
- **Find and close the right deal**
- **Generate cash flow forever**
- **Create generational wealth**
- **Start your path to freedom**

KP

Kuvaal Patel is a sales trainer, professional coach, and business leader in southern California. He built his first million-dollar organization before he turned 23.

From educators saying that he might not succeed, to being diagnosed with a learning disability, to graduating from the University of Arizona two years early, Kuvaal wants to help others create and live the life of their dreams.

His passions include real estate investing, personal growth and coaching, professional sports, and he is a professional model and actor.

Kuvaal wants to make sure that everyone knows what they can do to grow and build financial security for their future

HARD WORK MAY PAY IMMEDIATELY, BUT HARD-WORKING MONEY WILL PAY INDEFINITELY.
- KUVAAL PATEL

Zero to Ca$hflow

ZERO TO CA$HFLOW

KP

www.ingramcontent.com/pod-product-compliance
Lightning Source LLC
Chambersburg PA
CBHW020604220526
45463CB00006B/2444